A Piece of Cake

Sweet and Simple Quilts from Layer Cake Squares

PETA PEACE

Martingale
Create with Confidence

A Piece of Cake:
Sweet and Simple Quilts from Layer Cake Squares
© 2017 by Peta Peace

Martingale®
19021 120th Ave. NE, Ste. 102
Bothell, WA 98011-9511 USA
ShopMartingale.com

Printed in China
22 21 20 19 18 17   8 7 6 5 4 3 2 1

Library of Congress Cataloging-in-Publication Data
is available upon request.

ISBN: 978-1-60468-857-3

MISSION STATEMENT

We empower makers who use fabric and yarn
to make life more enjoyable.

CREDITS

PUBLISHER AND
CHIEF VISIONARY OFFICER
Jennifer Erbe Keltner

CONTENT DIRECTOR
Karen Costello Soltys

DESIGN MANAGER
Adrienne Smitke

MANAGING EDITOR
Tina Cook

PRODUCTION MANAGER
Regina Girard

ACQUISITIONS EDITOR
Karen M. Burns

PHOTOGRAPHER
Brent Kane

TECHNICAL EDITOR
Rebecca Kemp Brent

ILLUSTRATOR
Anne Moscicki

COPY EDITOR
Durby Peterson

DEDICATION

*To Richard, the best husband and friend a girl could have,
and to our beautiful kids, Georgia and Shelby*

Contents

Introduction

These days there is a wide and wonderful assortment of quilting fabric readily available for anyone who wants to make a quilt. Sounds great, right? It sure is, but it can also make the process of choosing fabric for a quilt a little overwhelming. Thankfully, Moda Fabrics and a number of other companies introduced precut fabric bundles several years ago and made all of our lives much easier.

Precut bundles contain at least one of each print in a fabric collection, depending on the type of bundle. There is quite an array of bundles on the market, and I truly love them all, but Layer Cakes—stacks of precut squares—are the ones I reach for most often. They contain about 42 squares (the number of squares may vary), each 10" × 10". Layer Cakes make it affordable to have pieces of all the fabrics in a collection, and their size allows you to cut them into any number of combinations to make a quilt.

All of the projects in *A Piece of Cake* are made with precut squares, but that doesn't mean that you must use *only* precut squares. If you have a bundle of fat eighths or fat quarters handy, you can just as easily use that, or if you're like me and have a healthy fabric collection, you could even cut 10" squares from your stash.

Some of the projects in this book are fast to make, such as Modern Spools (page 15) and Wrapped in Love (page 33). Some feature fresh twists on traditional blocks, such as Confetti (page 19), and some are just plain fun! All are designed to help build your skills as a quilter while you make beautiful quilted memories to cherish and share. I'm sure you'll find something you love.

XO,

Peta

Playing Around Again, pieced by Peta Peace and quilted by Diane Farrugia

FINISHED QUILT: 64½" × 80½" • **FINISHED BLOCK: 16" × 16"**

Playing Around Again

I love big-block quilts, especially when the blocks are simple, like the one used in Playing Around Again. They making sewing a quilt fast and fun—perfect for when you're short on time but need a good-sized quilt.

Materials

Yardage is based on 42"-wide fabric.

- 2¼ yards of white solid for background
- 80 precut squares, 10" × 10", of assorted prints for blocks
- ½ yard of pink print for binding
- 5 yards of fabric for backing
- 72" × 88" piece of batting

Cutting

From the white solid, cut:
18 strips, 4½" × 42"; crosscut into 160 squares, 4½" × 4½"

From *each* of the 80 precut squares, cut:
1 rectangle, 4½" × 8½" (80 total)
1 square, 4½" × 4½" (80 total)

From the pink print, cut:
7 strips, 2½" × 42"

Block Assembly

Use ¼" seam allowances. Press the seam allowances after each step as indicated by the arrows.

Refer to "Easy Corner Triangles and Flying Geese" on page 75 for details as needed.

1. Draw a diagonal line from corner to corner on the wrong side of 80 white squares.

2. For one block, choose four assorted rectangles plus a matching square for each. You'll also need eight white squares (four marked and four unmarked).

3. Place a marked white square on top of a print rectangle, right sides together. Pin the white square in place and sew on the drawn line. Trim ¼" outside the sewn line. Make one of

Pick and Choose

Sewing with precut squares is convenient, but sometimes you might find that a few prints are a little too light or too dark or don't quite suit the look of your quilt. Swapping misfit squares for prints you have in your stash is a great way to personalize and add flair to the quilt. You might even like to add some fabrics that have a particular meaning to you or to the recipient of the quilt.

each print, two with the seam slanted as in A and two as in B below. Press, noting that not all are pressed toward the print.

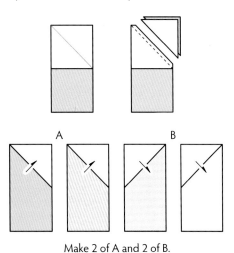

Make 2 of A and 2 of B.

4. With right sides together, sew an unmarked white square to each print square.

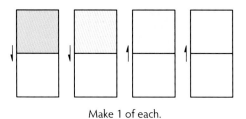

Make 1 of each.

5. Sew a unit from step 3 to a unit from step 4, keeping like prints together, to make a quarter-block unit. Make four, one of each print; each quarter-block unit should measure 8½" square, including the seam allowances. Notice

that two units have the squares on the left, while the other two have them on the right.

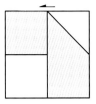 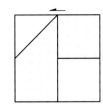

Unit A.
Make 2 per block,
8½" × 8½".

Unit B.
Make 2 per block,
8½" × 8½".

6. Arrange the quarter blocks as shown, with the white triangles in the center of the block and the white squares in the outer corners. Sew the quarter blocks together to make two rows. Sew the rows together to complete the block. Make 20 blocks measuring 16½" square, including the seam allowances.

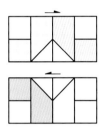 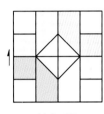

Make 20,
16½" × 16½".

Quilt Assembly

1. Arrange the blocks, rotating them as necessary so the seam allowances nest, into five rows of four blocks each. Sew the blocks into rows. Press the seam allowances in opposite directions from row to row. Each row should measure 16½" × 64½", including the seam allowances.

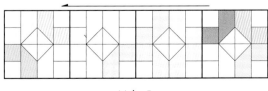

Make 5,
16½" × 64½".

2. Sew the rows together and press the seam allowances open as shown. The quilt top should measure 64½" × 80½".

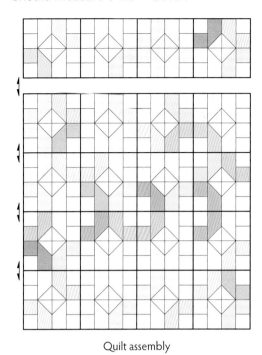

Quilt assembly

Finishing the Quilt

Refer to "Finishing Your Quilt" on page 76 for details as needed.

1. Trim the selvages from the backing fabric and cut the backing into two pieces, approximately 42" × 90" each. Prepare the backing as instructed in "Making the Quilt Backing" on page 76. Trim to approximately 72" × 88" for a backing with a vertical seam.

2. Layer the quilt top with batting and backing. Baste the layers together and quilt as desired. The quilt shown is machine quilted with an allover loop design.

3. Bind the edges with the 2½"-wide pink strips. Add a label to your quilt, if desired.

A Piece of Cake, pieced by Peta Peace and quilted by Diane Farrugia

FINISHED QUILT: 64½" × 72½" • FINISHED BLOCK: 8" × 8"

A Piece of Cake

Precut squares are perfect for quick and easy quilts. You slice them just like a piece of sheet cake, and voilà! In no time at all you have a simple yet striking quilt ready to be used and loved. This easy-to-sew block is perfect for bright, bold prints. Or, team soft, pretty colors with a quiet feature print for a different look.

Cutting

From the black polka dot, cut:
9 strips, 2½" × 42"; crosscut into 18 rectangles, 2½" × 21"
7 strips, 2½" × 42"*

From the white solid, cut:
5 strips, 8½" × 42"; crosscut into 72 rectangles, 2½" × 8½"
5 strips, 4½" × 42"; crosscut into 9 rectangles, 4½" × 21"

From *each* of the 36 precut squares, cut:
2 rectangles, 4½" × 8½" (72 total)

*If your fabric runs narrow, you may need to cut an extra strip.

Materials

Yardage is based on 42"-wide fabric.

- 1⅜ yards of black polka dot for blocks and binding
- 2 yards of white solid for blocks
- 36 precut squares, 10" × 10", of assorted prints for blocks
- 4⅛ yards of fabric for backing
- 72" × 80" piece of batting

Cut Them in Half

I always cut my strips into two 21" lengths for strip piecing. It's much easier to keep the shorter lengths aligned correctly when chain piecing. Pressing them is easier too.

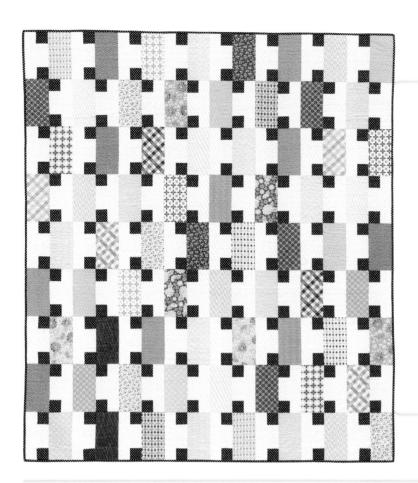

Easy Resizing

You should have enough leftover squares from the Layer Cake to cut eight more rectangles to make the quilt one row (8") longer. If you need it wider, you'll need to make nine more blocks, one for each row, to make a 72½" square quilt. You'll need five additional 10" squares to yield nine more print rectangles. If you don't have enough precut squares, you can always add a square or two from your stash!

Block Assembly

Use ¼" seam allowances. Press the seam allowances after each step as indicated by the arrows.

1. Sew 2½" × 21" polka-dot strips to the long edges of a 4½" × 21" white strip. Make nine strip sets, 8½" × 21". Crosscut each strip set into eight 2½" × 8½" segments (72 total).

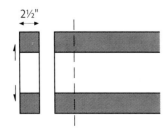

Make 9 strip sets. Cut 8 segments from each (72 total).

2. Sew a strip-set segment to the left edge of a print 4½" × 8½" rectangle to make a 6½" × 8½" unit.

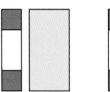

3. Sew a 2½" × 8½" white rectangle to the free edge of the strip-set unit. Make 72 blocks. The blocks should measure 8½" square, including the seam allowances.

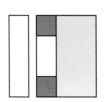

Make 72, 8½" × 8½".

Quilt Assembly

1. Referring to the quilt assembly diagram below, arrange the blocks, alternating the orientation of each row, in nine rows of eight blocks.

2. Sew the blocks into rows. Press the seam allowances in opposite directions from row to row. Each row should measure 8½" × 64½", including the seam allowances.

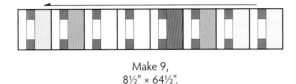

Make 9,
8½" × 64½".

3. Sew the rows together. The quilt top should measure 64½" × 72½".

Finishing the Quilt

Refer to "Finishing Your Quilt" on page 76 for details as needed.

1. Trim the selvages from the backing fabric and cut the backing into two pieces, approximately 42" × 72" each. Prepare the backing as instructed in "Making the Quilt Backing" on page 76. Trim to approximately 72" × 80" for a backing with a horizontal seam.

2. Layer the quilt top with batting and backing. Baste and then quilt as desired. The quilt shown is machine quilted with an allover elongated loop pattern.

3. Bind the edges with the 2½"-wide polka-dot strips. Add a label to your quilt, if desired.

Quilt assembly

Modern Spools, pieced by Peta Peace and quilted by Diane Farrugia

FINISHED QUILT: 38½" × 42½" • **FINISHED BLOCK: 5" × 9"**

Modern Spools

I've always loved traditional Spool quilts, but their blocks don't look much like the spools of thread readily available in my homeland of Australia. I also love pictures of thread on spools lined up in neat rows, looking perfect and pretty. Whenever I try to re-create those displays, one of the spools always falls over! I designed Modern Spools with a fresh, updated Spool block that's quick and easy to piece using a stack of precut squares or scraps you have at home.

Materials

Yardage is based on 42"-wide fabric. Fat quarters measure 18" × 21".

- 1 yard of white solid for blocks, sashing, and border
- 1 fat quarter of gray print for spool ends
- 23 precut squares, 10" × 10", of assorted prints for blocks
- ⅜ yard of blue print for binding
- 2⅝ yards of fabric for backing
- 46" × 50" piece of batting

Cutting

From the white solid, cut:
4 strips, 1¾" × 42"; crosscut into 8 strips,
    1¾" × 21"
1 strip, 9½" × 42"; crosscut into:
    19 strips, 1½" × 9½"
    1 square, 9½" × 9½"
3 strips, 1½" × 35½"
1 square, 6½" × 6½"
2 strips, 2" × 39½"
2 strips, 2" × 38½"

From the gray print, cut:
4 strips, 3" × 21"

From *each* of the 23 precut squares, cut:
1 rectangle, 5½" × 7½" (23 total)

From the blue print, cut:
5 strips, 2½" × 42"

Spool Block Assembly

Use ¼" seam allowances. Press the seam allowances after each step as indicated by the arrows.

1. Sew white 1¾" × 21" strips to the long edges of a gray 3" × 21" strip. Make four strip sets measuring 5½" × 21".

2. Crosscut each strip set into 13 segments, 1½" × 5½" (52 total).

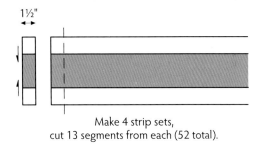

1½"

Make 4 strip sets,
cut 13 segments from each (52 total).

3. Sew segments to the short ends of a 5½" × 7½" print rectangle. Make 23 blocks measuring 5½" × 9½", including the seam allowances.

Make 23,
5½" × 9½".

Tilted-Spool Block Assembly

1. Cut the 9½" white square in half diagonally to yield two triangles.

2. Center the triangles on the long edges of one Spool block and sew with right sides together.

Trim the dog-ears to straighten the top and bottom edges.

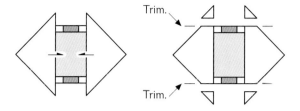

3. Cut the 6½" white square in half diagonally to yield two triangles. Center the triangles on the top and bottom of the Spool block and sew with right sides together. Fold the block in half diagonally (along the lengthwise center of the spool) and press lightly to crease.

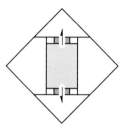

4. Align the crease with the 45° mark on a rotary-cutting ruler and trim the block to measure 9½" high and 11½" wide, with the top of the spool tilted to the right. Before trimming, be sure that there is ¼" seam allowance inside the circled area as shown.

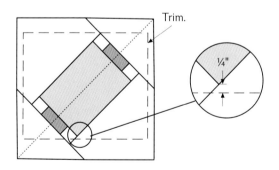

Quilt Assembly

1. Arrange the blocks and sashing strips as shown in the quilt assembly diagram. Sew the blocks and 1½" × 9½" vertical sashing strips

together into four rows measuring 9½" × 35½", including the seam allowances.

2. Sew the pieced rows and horizontal sashing strips together. The quilt center should measure 35½" × 39½", including the seam allowances.

3. Sew the 2" × 39½" white strips to the sides of the quilt center. Sew the 2" × 38½" white strips to the top and bottom edges of the quilt. The quilt top should measure 38½" × 42½".

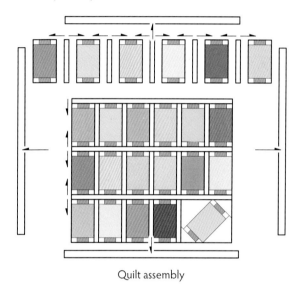

Quilt assembly

Finishing the Quilt

Refer to "Finishing Your Quilt" on page 76 for details as needed.

1. Trim the selvages from the backing fabric and cut the backing into two pieces, approximately 42" × 47" each. Prepare the backing as instructed in "Making the Quilt Backing" on page 76. Trim to approximately 46" × 50" for a backing with a horizontal seam.

2. Layer the quilt top with batting and backing, and baste. Quilt as desired. The quilt shown is machine quilted in an allover meandering pattern.

3. Bind the edges with the 2½"-wide blue strips. Add a label to your quilt, if desired.

Confetti, pieced by Peta Peace and quilted by Diane Farrugia

FINISHED QUILT: 52½" × 64½" • FINISHED BLOCKS: 8" × 8" and 8" × 12"

We have plenty of girls in our family, so there's always room for another sweet and pretty quilt like this one. If you have a bevy of boys in your family, grab a stack of precut squares in boy-themed prints and darker background fabric. The outcome will look just as good!

Materials

Yardage is based on 42"-wide fabric.

- 44 precut squares, 10" × 10", of assorted prints for blocks
- 2⅝ yards of white solid for background
- ½ yard of fabric *OR* leftover assorted prints for binding*
- 3⅜ yards of fabric for backing
- 60" × 72" piece of batting

If you use assorted prints, cut 2½"-wide strips to total 242" for a pieced binding as shown on page 20.

Cutting

From *each* of 20 precut squares (Star blocks), cut:
1 square, 4½" × 4½" (20 total)
8 squares, 2½" × 2½" (160 total)

From *each* of 20 precut squares (Streamer blocks), cut:
1 rectangle, 4½" × 8½" (20 total)
4 squares, 2½" × 2½" (80 total)

From *each* of the remaining 4 precut squares (Short Streamer blocks), cut:
4 rectangles, 2½" × 4½" (16 total)

From the white solid, cut:
3 strips, 12½" × 42"; crosscut into 40 strips, 2½" × 12½"
8 strips, 4½" × 42"; crosscut into 120 rectangles, 2½" × 4½"
6 strips, 2½" × 42"; crosscut into 96 squares, 2½" × 2½"

From the binding fabric, cut:
6 strips, 2½" × 42", *OR* 26 strips, 2½" × 10"

Scrappy Binding from Precut Squares

If you're careful when cutting the precut 10" squares into the patchwork pieces, you should have enough left over to cut 2½" × 10" strips that you can piece together to make a scrappy binding, as on the quilt shown. You'll need approximately 26 strips for the scrappy binding.

Star Block Assembly

Use ¼" seam allowances. Press the seam allowances after each step as indicated by the arrows.

Use one print per block; instructions are for one block. Refer to "Easy Corner Triangles and Flying Geese" on page 75 for details as needed.

1. Draw a diagonal line from corner to corner on the wrong side of eight 2½" print squares.

2. Place a marked square on a 2½" × 4½" white rectangle with right sides together, orienting the line as shown. Pin the square in place and sew on the drawn line. Trim ¼" outside the sewn line, and then press the resulting triangle open.

3. Place a second marked square on the opposite end of the rectangle, orienting the line as shown. Pin the square in place and sew on the drawn line. Trim ¼" outside the sewn line. Make four flying-geese units measuring 2½" × 4½", including the seam allowances.

Make 4,
2½" × 4½".

4. Arrange the four flying-geese units, one 4½" print square, and four 2½" white squares as shown. Sew the units together to make three rows; then sew the rows together to make one block. Make 20. The blocks should measure 8½" square, including the seam allowances.

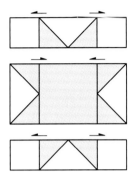 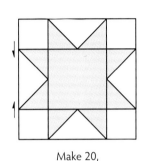

Make 20,
8½" × 8½".

Streamer Block Assembly

Use one print per block.

1. Follow steps 1–3 of "Star Block Assembly" to mark four 2½" print squares and make two flying-geese units measuring 2½" × 4½", including the seam allowances.

2. Sew flying-geese units to the short ends of the 4½" × 8½" matching-print rectangle. Sew 2½" × 12½" white strips to the top and bottom of the unit. Repeat to make 20 blocks. The completed blocks should measure 8½" × 12½", including the seam allowances.

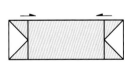 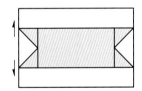

Make 20,
8½" × 12½".

Short Streamer Block Assembly

Use one print per block; make two blocks from each print.

1. Draw a diagonal line from corner to corner on the wrong side of two 2½" white squares.

2. Place a marked square on a 2½" × 4½" print rectangle with right sides together, orienting the line as shown. Pin the square in place and sew on the drawn line. Trim ¼" outside the sewn line.

3. Make a second rectangle unit with its seam oriented in the opposite direction.

Make 1 of each.

4. Sew the two rectangle units together, ensuring that the white triangles are oriented correctly. Make eight. The completed blocks should measure 2½" × 8½", including the seam allowances.

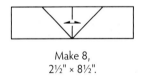

Make 8,
2½" × 8½".

Rule Breaker

Sometimes it pays to press seam allowances toward the lighter fabric so that the seams nest, creating a flatter block overall.

Quilt Assembly

1. Arrange three Streamer blocks and two Star blocks in a row as shown. Sew them together to make row A. Make four. The rows should measure 8½" × 52½", including the seam allowances.

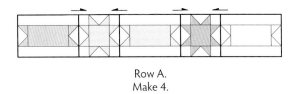

Row A.
Make 4.

2. Arrange two Short Streamer blocks, three Star blocks, and two Streamer blocks in a row as shown. Sew them together to complete row B. Make four. The rows should measure 8½" × 52½", including the seam allowances.

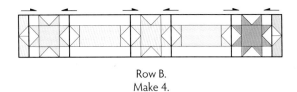

Row B.
Make 4.

3. Sew the rows together, alternating A and B from top to bottom. Match the seam intersections as you sew. The quilt top should measure 52½" × 64½".

Finishing the Quilt

Refer to "Finishing Your Quilt" on page 76 for details as needed.

1. Trim the selvages from the backing fabric and cut the backing into two pieces, approximately 42" × 61" each. Prepare the backing as instructed in "Making the Quilt Backing" on page 76. Trim to approximately 60" × 72" for a backing with a horizontal seam.

2. Layer the quilt top with batting and backing. Baste and then quilt as desired. The quilt shown is machine quilted in an allover pattern of swirls and curls.

3. Bind the edges with the 2½"-wide assorted print strips. Add a label to your quilt, if desired.

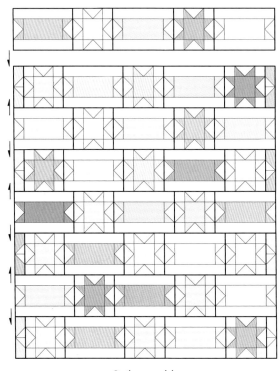

Quilt assembly

Who doesn't remember spinning around in circles as a kid until you were dizzy? That was such good fun. These days my fun looks a little different: usually it has three layers, pretty fabric, and some pieces sewn together into simple blocks! The best part comes afterward, snuggling under the quilt to watch movies.

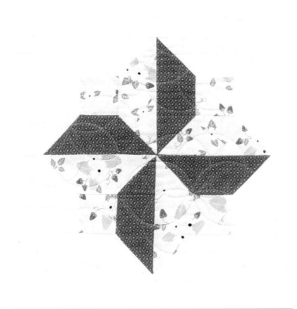

Materials

Yardage is based on 42"-wide fabric.

- 2⅝ yards of white solid for background, sashing, and inner border
- 32 precut squares, 10" × 10", of assorted prints for blocks
- ½ yard of pink print for middle border
- ⅝ yard of raspberry print for outer border
- ⅝ yard of blue print for binding
- 4⅛ yards of fabric for backing
- 74" × 74" piece of batting

Cutting

From the white solid, cut:
34 strips, 2½" × 42"; crosscut *24 strips* into:
    192 squares, 2½" × 2½"
    64 rectangles, 2½" × 4½"
    12 strips, 2½" × 12½"

From *each* of 16 of the precut squares (main prints), cut:
4 squares, 2½" × 2½" (64 total)
4 rectangles, 2½" × 6½" (64 total)

From *each* of the remaining 16 precut squares (accent prints), cut:
4 rectangles, 2½" × 4½" (64 total)
4 squares, 2½" × 2½" (64 total)

From the pink print, cut:
6 strips, 2½" × 42

From the raspberry print, cut:
7 strips, 2½" × 42

From the blue print, cut:
7 strips, 2½" × 42"

Spin, pieced by Peta Peace and quilted by Diane Farrugia

FINISHED QUILT: 66½" × 66½" • FINISHED BLOCK: 12" × 12"

Block Assembly

Use ¼" seam allowances. Press the seam allowances after each step as indicated by the arrows.

Use a single main print and a single accent print in each block. Instructions are for one block. Refer to "Easy Corner Triangles and Flying Geese" on page 75 for details as needed.

1. Draw a diagonal line from corner to corner on the wrong side of eight white 2½" squares and four 2½" accent squares.

2. Pin a marked white square on a 2½" × 4½" accent rectangle with right sides together, orienting the drawn line as shown. Sew on the drawn line. Trim ¼" outside the drawn line. Make four.

 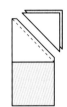 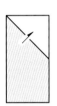

3. Sew an unmarked white 2½" square to a main-print 2½" square. Sew a white 2½" × 4½" rectangle to the top of the unit, keeping the colors in the correct positions. Make four.

 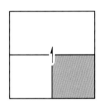

4. Keeping the colors in the correct positions, sew together one unit from step 2 and one unit from step 3.

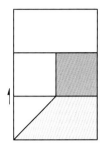

5. Place a marked white square on a main-print 2½" × 6½" rectangle with right sides together, orienting the line as shown. Pin, sew, and trim as before. Repeat to add a marked square of the accent print to the other end of the rectangle, paying close attention to the direction of the seamline. Make four.

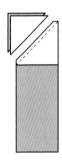  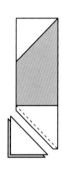 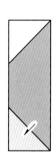

6. Sew the units from steps 4 and 5 together to complete a quarter block measuring 6½" square, including the seam allowances. Make four.

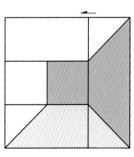

Make 4,
6½" × 6½".

Mix Things Up

While I combined some busy prints in my blocks, the overall look of the quilt is a bit on the muted side. You can spice things up with brighter prints, or consider using a solid color in place of one of the prints in each block for extra pop.

7. Arrange the quarter blocks, rotating the units as necessary. Sew the blocks together in pairs and then join the pairs to make a block measuring 12½" square, including the seam allowances. Make 16 blocks.

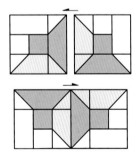
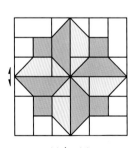

Make 16,
12½" × 12½".

Quilt Assembly

1. Sew seven 2½" × 42" white strips together end to end to make a long strip for the horizontal sashing and horizontal inner border. Press the seam allowances open. From this long strip, cut five strips, 2½" × 54½".

2. Arrange the blocks, 2½" × 12½" vertical sashing strips, and three of the 2½" × 54½" horizontal strips as shown in the quilt assembly diagram on page 27.

3. Sew the blocks and sashing strips together into rows. Sew the rows and horizontal sashing strips together. The quilt center should measure 54½" square, including the seam allowances.

Adding the Borders

For detailed instructions, refer to "Borders" on page 76.

1. Sew the two remaining white 2½" × 54½" strips to the top and bottom of the quilt. Join the remaining three white 2½" × 42" strips together end to end and press the seam allowances open. From the pieced strip, cut two strips, 2½" × 58½". Sew these borders to the top and bottom of the quilt.

2. Sew the six pink 2½" × 42" strips together end to end to make one long strip. Press the seam allowances open. Cut two strips, 2½" × 58½", and sew them to the sides of the quilt. Cut two more strips, 2½" × 62½", and sew them to the top and bottom of the quilt.

3. Sew the seven raspberry 2½" × 42" strips together end to end to make one long strip. Press the seam allowances open. From the pieced strip, cut two strips, 2½" × 62½", and sew them to the sides of the quilt. Cut two more strips, 2½" × 66½", and sew them to the top and bottom edges of the quilt. The quilt top should measure 66½" square.

Finishing the Quilt

Refer to "Finishing Your Quilt" on page 76 for details as needed.

1. Trim the selvages from the backing fabric and cut the backing into two pieces, approximately 42" × 74" each. Prepare the backing as instructed in "Making the Quilt Backing" on page 76. Trim to approximately 74" square for a backing with a vertical seam.

2. Layer the quilt top with batting and backing. Baste and quilt as desired. The quilt shown is quilted with an allover circle design.

3. Bind the edges with the blue 2½"-wide strips. Add a label to your quilt, if desired.

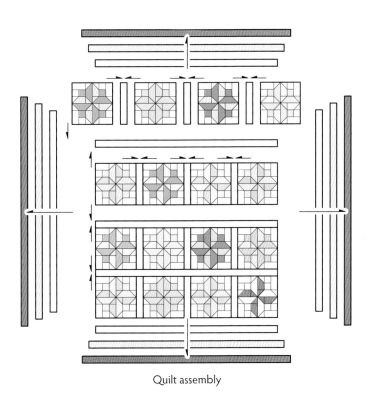

Quilt assembly

Spin Pillow, pieced and quilted by Peta Peace

FINISHED PILLOW: 16½" × 16½"

When there's no time to spare, a sweet pillow makes a great gift. Use leftover precut squares from the Spin quilt on page 23 to make this one-block pillow top in no time at all!

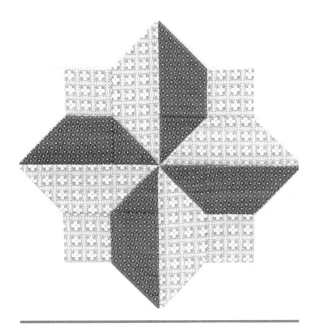

- 18" × 18" piece of muslin for quilt backing*
- 18" × 18" piece of batting
- 14" coordinating zipper
- 16" pillow form

*If you don't have muslin handy, you could also use an 18" × 18" piece of white solid for the quilt backing.

Materials

Yardage is based on 42"-wide fabric. Fat quarters measure 18" × 21"; fat eighths, 9" × 21".

- 2 precut squares, 10" × 10", of coordinating prints for block
- 1 fat eighth of white solid for background
- ½ yard of raspberry print for border and pillow back
- ⅛ yard of fusible interfacing
- 1 fat quarter of pink print for binding

Cutting

From 1 precut square (main fabric), cut:
4 squares, 2½" × 2½"
4 rectangles, 2½" × 6½"

From the remaining precut square (accent fabric), cut:
4 rectangles, 2½" × 4½"
4 squares, 2½" × 2½"

From the white solid, cut:
3 strips, 2½" × 21"; crosscut into:
    12 squares, 2½" × 2½"
    4 rectangles, 2½" × 4½"

From the raspberry print, cut:
2 strips, 2½" × 12½"
2 strips, 2½" × 16½"
2 rectangles, 9½" × 17"

From the pink print, cut:
4 strips, 2½" × 21"

From the fusible interfacing, cut:
2 strips, 1½" × 17"

Block Assembly

Follow the steps in "Block Assembly" on page 25 to make one Spin block.

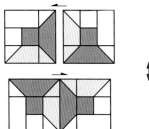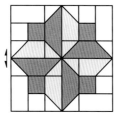

Adding the Border

Use ¼" seam allowances. Press the seam allowances after each step as indicated by the arrows.

For detailed instructions, refer to "Borders" on page 76.

1. Sew the 2½" × 12½" raspberry strips to the top and bottom of the Spin block.

2. Sew the 2½" × 16½" raspberry strips to the sides of the pillow front. The pillow front should measure 16½" square, including the seam allowances.

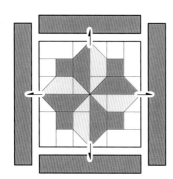

Finishing the Pillow

Refer to "Finishing Your Quilt" on page 76 for details as needed.

1. Layer the pillow front with the batting and the muslin square. Baste and quilt as desired. The sample is stitched in the ditch.

2. Following the manufacturer's instructions, attach a strip of fusible interfacing to the wrong side of each pillow-back rectangle along one 17" edge. Place the backing pieces on a flat surface, right side down, so that the interfaced edges are touching and the sides are aligned. Mark the start and end of the zipper on both pieces of fabric and then make a small snip into the seam allowance at each mark.

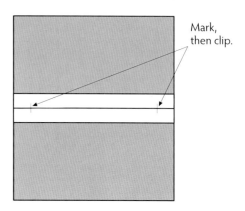

Mark, then clip.

3. Pin the raspberry backing rectangles right sides together with the snips aligned. Using a ⅝" seam allowance and standard stitch length (10 to 12 stitches per inch, or 2.5 mm), sew from one side edge to the nearest snip, and then backstitch. Change the stitch to a basting length (about 6 stitches per inch, or 4 mm) and continue sewing to the second snip. Change the stitch length to standard length, sew a few stitches, and then backstitch to the snip. Continue sewing with a standard stitch length to the edge. Press the seam allowances open and flat.

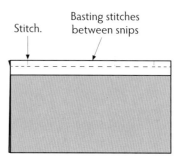

Stitch.

Basting stitches between snips

4. Place the zipper right side down on the seam allowance of one backing rectangle, aligning the ends of the zipper teeth with the snips. Position the zipper teeth on the seamline. Fold the other layers of the backing out of the way and stitch the zipper to the seam allowance only, sewing close to the zipper teeth (about ⅛" from the seamline).

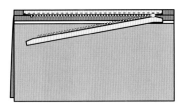

5. Fold the seam allowance and zipper tape behind the other layers, forming a tuck in the seam allowance, and pin in place. Sew through the folded seam allowance and the zipper tape close to the basted seam, being careful not to sew through other parts of the backing.

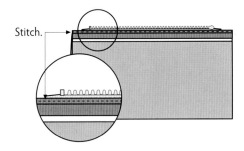

Stitch.

6. Smooth the pillow back flat, with the seam allowances open and the zipper spread on top of both seam allowances. The tuck in the seam allowance will shift the zipper teeth slightly away from the basted seam. Pin through the layers near the zipper ends (marked with snips). Working from the right side, sew through the pillow back, seam allowances,

and zipper tape from the seamline to the other side of the zipper teeth (about ⅜"). With the needle down, lift the presser foot and pivot to stitch along the zipper, parallel to the basted seam. Stop at the pin mark, pivot again, and stitch to the seamline. Backstitch at the beginning and end of the topstitching.

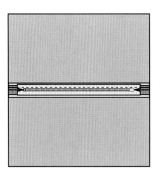

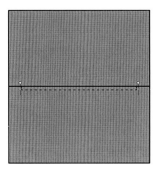

7. Use a seam ripper to open the basted section of the seam. Trim the pillow back to 16½" square.

8. Place the pillow top and back *wrong* sides together, aligning the raw edges, with the zipper running from side to side. Pin in place and then baste around all four sides, ⅛" from the raw edges.

9. Bind the edges with the 2½"-wide pink strips. Add a label to your pillow, if desired.

Wrapped in Love, pieced by Peta Peace and quilted by Fiona Bell

FINISHED QUILT: 45" × 50" • FINISHED BLOCKS: 15" × 20" and 20" × 20"

Wrapped in Love

I'm a sucker for anything love related, and I'm also a sucker for quilts that send a message. Wrapped in Love combines both qualities in a sweet quilt that's the perfect quick weekend project for a new baby you love.

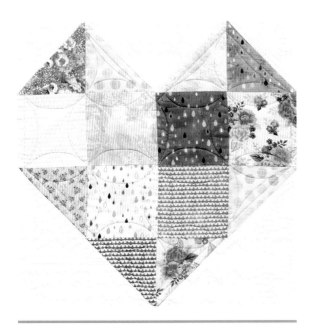

Materials

Yardage is based on 42"-wide fabric.

- 1½ yards of white solid for blocks, sashing, and border
- 32 precut squares, 10" × 10", of assorted prints for blocks
- ½ yard of orange print for binding
- 3 yards of fabric for backing
- 53" × 58" piece of batting

Cutting

Save the leftovers from cutting this project to make the mini version on page 37.

From the white solid, cut:

1 strip, 10½" × 42"; crosscut into:
    1 rectangle, 10½" × 15½" (L block)
    1 rectangle, 5½" × 10½" (E block)
    1 square, 10½" × 10½"
    1 square, 6¼" × 6¼"
1 strip, 6¼" × 42"; crosscut into 6 squares,
    6¼" × 6¼"
1 strip, 5½" × 42"; crosscut into:
    4 squares, 5½" × 5½" (Heart block, V block)
    2 rectangles, 3" × 5½"
1 strip, 3" × 42"; crosscut into 2 strips, 3" × 20½"
1 strip, 3" × 38"
2 strips, 4" × 38"
3 strips, 4" × 42"

From *each* of 25 of the precut squares, cut:

1 square, 5½" × 5½" (25 total)

From *each* of the remaining 7 precut squares, cut:

1 square, 6¼" × 6¼" (7 total)

From the orange print, cut:

5 strips, 2½" × 42"

Wrapped in Love is the perfect quilt to welcome a new baby, but at 45" × 50" it also makes a nice lap quilt for a child or a display quilt for a wall. What a wonderful way to remind special children just how much they're loved!

Block Assembly

Use ¼" seam allowances. Press the seam allowances after each step as indicated by the arrows.

Refer to "Half-Square Triangles" on page 74 for details as needed.

1. Draw a diagonal line from corner to corner on the wrong side of the seven 6¼" white squares.

2. Place a marked square on a 6¼" print square with right sides together. Pin the white square in place and sew a scant ¼" from both sides of the drawn line. Cut on the drawn line to yield two half-square-triangle units. Make 14. Trim to 5½" square.

Make 14.

L BLOCK

You'll need six 5½" print squares and the 10½" × 15½" white rectangle.

1. Sew three 5½" print squares together to make a 5½" × 15½" strip. Make two.

2. Sew the 10½" × 15½" white rectangle to the right edge of a pieced unit. Sew the remaining pieced strip to the bottom of the unit. The L block should measure 15½" × 20½", including the seam allowances.

 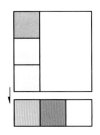

15½" × 20½"

HEART BLOCK

You'll need six 5½" print squares, eight half-square-triangle units, and two 5½" white squares.

1. Arrange the squares and half-square-triangle units as shown, paying careful attention to the orientation of the seams between triangles.

2. Sew the pieces together in rows, alternating the pressing direction from row to row. Join the rows to make the block. The Heart block should measure 20½" square, including the seam allowances.

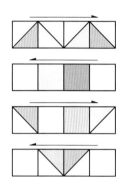 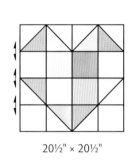

20½" × 20½"

V BLOCK

You'll need four 5½" print squares, six half-square-triangle units, and the 10½" white square.

1. Sew two 5½" print squares together to make a 5½" × 10½" unit. Make two.

2. Sew the pieced units to opposite sides of the 10½" white square to make the top half of the block.

 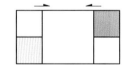

3. Arrange the remaining squares and half-square-triangle units as shown, paying careful attention to the seam directions and print placement. Sew the units together in rows, pressing as shown, and then join the rows to make the bottom half of the block.

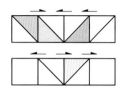 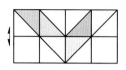

4. Sew the two halves of the block together. The V block should measure 20½" square, including the seam allowances.

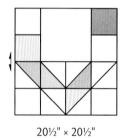

20½" × 20½"

E BLOCK

You'll need nine 5½" print squares, two 3" × 5½" white rectangles, and one 5½" × 10½" white rectangle.

1. Sew two 5½" print squares together to make a 5½" × 10½" unit. Make two.

2. Sew four 5½" print squares together to make a 5½" × 20½" strip.

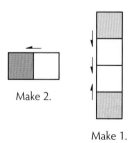

Make 2.

Make 1.

3. Sew 3" × 5½" white rectangles to the top and bottom of the remaining 5½" print square. Stitch the 5½" × 10½" white rectangle to the right edge of the unit. Sew the two-square units from step 1 to the top and bottom.

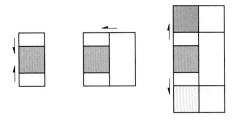

4. Sew the four-square strip from step 2 to the left edge of the unit to complete the E block, which should measure 15½" × 20½", including the seam allowances.

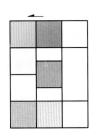

15½" × 20½"

Quilt Assembly

For detailed instructions, refer to "Borders" on page 76.

1. Arrange the blocks and 3" × 20½" white rectangles in two rows as shown. Sew together the pieces in each row. Each row should measure 20½" × 38", including the seam allowances.

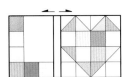 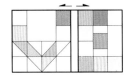

2. Sew the rows together with the 3" × 38" white strip between them. The quilt center should measure 38" × 43", including the seam allowances.

3. Sew the 4" × 38" white strips to the top and bottom of the quilt center. Join the three 4" × 42" white strips end to end to make one long strip. From the pieced strip, cut two strips, 4" × 50", and sew them to the sides of the quilt center. The finished quilt top should measure 45" × 50".

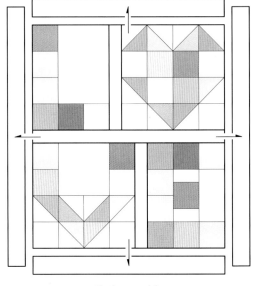

Quilt assembly

Finishing the Quilt

Refer to "Finishing Your Quilt" on page 76 for details as needed.

1. Trim the selvages from the backing fabric and cut the backing into two pieces, approximately 42" × 54" each. Prepare the backing as instructed in "Making the Quilt Backing" on page 76. Trim to approximately 53" × 58" to make a backing with a horizontal seam.

2. Layer the quilt top with batting and backing. Baste the quilt sandwich and quilt as desired. The quilt shown is machine quilted with a variety of loops, swirls, and diagonal lines.

3. Bind the edges with the 2½"-wide orange strips. Add a label to your quilt, if desired.

Make It Mini!

Use leftovers from your precut squares to make a miniaturized version of the Wrapped in Love quilt.

FINISHED QUILT: 18½" × 20½"

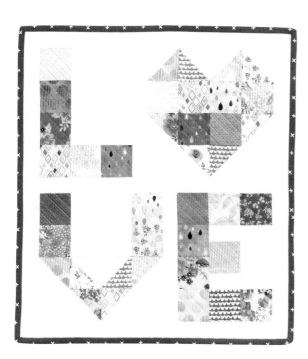

Materials

Yardage is based on 42"-wide fabric. Fat quarters measure 18" × 21".

- 25 squares, 2½" × 2½", of assorted prints for blocks
- 7 squares, 3¼" × 3¼", of assorted prints for blocks
- ⅝ yard of white solid for blocks, sashing, and border
- 1 fat quarter of gray print for binding
- ⅝ yard of fabric for backing
- 22" × 22" square of batting

Cutting

From the white solid, cut:
1 strip, 4½" × 42"; crosscut into:
    1 rectangle, 4½" × 6½", for L block
    1 square, 4½" × 4½", for V block
    1 rectangle, 2½" × 4½", for E block
    7 squares, 3¼" × 3¼"
1 strip, 2½" × 42"; crosscut into:
    4 squares, 2½" × 2½", for V and Heart blocks
    2 rectangles, 1½" × 2½", for E block
3 strips, 2" × 42"; crosscut into:
    2 strips, 1½" × 8½", for vertical sashing
    1 strip, 1½" × 15½", for horizontal sashing
    2 strips, 2" × 15½", for top and bottom borders
    2 strips, 2" × 20½", for side borders

From the gray print, cut:
4 strips, 2¼" × 21"*

From the backing fabric, cut:
1 square, 22" × 22"

I recommend narrow binding on miniature quilts.

Quilt Assembly

Follow the steps shown in the Wrapped in Love quilt to make your mini-quilt!

Delight, pieced by Peta Peace and quilted by Diane Farrugia

FINISHED QUILT: 84½" × 84½" • **FINISHED BLOCK: 21" × 21"**

Delight

Every now and again a quilt show comes to town that showcases quilts from days gone by. My favorite quilts are always the ones that are made with hundreds of different fabrics; somehow those delightfully scrappy quilts look as if every piece was carefully selected, when in reality it was probably just a case of using what was available. Those quilts are an inspirational reminder to keep it simple and use some of that fabric we've all got sitting in the cupboard.

Cutting

From *each* of 64 of the precut squares, cut:
4 squares, 4¾" × 4¾" (256 total)

From *each* of the remaining 16 precut squares, cut:
2 squares, 4" × 4" (32 total)

From the white solid, cut:
24 strips, 4¾" × 42"; crosscut into 192 squares, 4¾" × 4¾"
7 strips, 4" × 42"; crosscut into 64 squares, 4" × 4"

From the pink print, cut:
9 strips, 2½" × 42"

Materials

Yardage is based on 42"-wide fabric.

- 80 precut squares, 10" × 10", of assorted prints for blocks
- 4⅛ yards of white solid for background
- ¾ yard of pink print for binding
- 7¾ yards of fabric for backing
- 92" × 92" piece of batting

Practically Perfect

Keep in mind that no quilt is perfect. No one is going to inspect and give you a score! It's far more likely that everyone who sees your quilt will love it, and if you give it to someone special, they'll love it even more because it was made with a whole lot of love by you!

Block Assembly

Use ¼" seam allowances. Press the seam allowances after each step as indicated by the arrows.

Each block is made up of half-square triangles and squares. Select six different prints for each block. Refer to "Half-Square Triangles" on page 74 for details as needed.

1. Using four 4¾" squares of the first print and four 4¾" white squares, make eight half-square-triangle units. Trim each unit to measure 4" square, including the seam allowances. Repeat to make eight units from a second print and white solid.

2. Use two 4¾" squares *each* of a third print and white solid to make four half-square-triangle units. Make four half-square-triangle units from the fourth print and white solid, and four

half-square-triangle units combining prints three and four. Trim all to measure 4" square, including the seam allowances.

Make 4 of each.

Make 4 of each.

3. Arrange the half-square-triangle units, two 4" squares *each* of the fifth and sixth prints, and four white 4" squares to make a block, paying careful attention to the orientation of each half-square-triangle unit and its seam allowances to ensure that the seams nest together.

4. Sew the units together in rows. Join the rows to complete the block. Make 16 blocks measuring 21½" square, including the seam allowances.

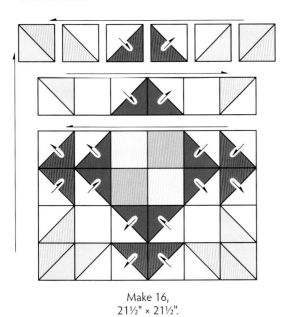

Make 16,
21½" × 21½".

Eight-Pointed Stars

Surprise! Did you think you'd be piecing Eight-Pointed Star blocks? Wondering where they are? They aren't formed until you join the blocks, creating the secondary pattern, which means piecing these blocks and the quilt top is much easier than it first appears.

Quilt Assembly

1. Arrange the blocks in four rows of four as shown. Rotate alternate blocks 180° to ensure that all of the seam allowances nest. Sew the blocks together into rows measuring 21½" × 84½", including the seam allowances.

2. Sew the rows together. The quilt top should measure 84½" square.

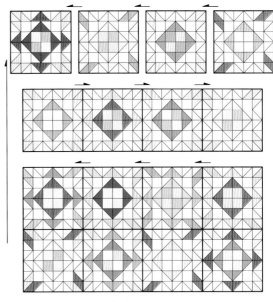

Quilt assembly

Finishing the Quilt

Refer to "Finishing Your Quilt" on page 76 for details as needed.

1. Trim the selvages from the backing fabric and cut the backing into three pieces, approximately 42" × 93" each. Prepare the backing as instructed in "Making the Quilt Backing" on page 76, using three pieces rather than two. Trim to approximately 92" square for a backing with horizontal seams.

2. Layer the quilt top with batting and backing and quilt as desired. The quilt shown is machine quilted with parallel diagonal lines.

3. Bind the edges with the pink 2½"-wide strips. Add a label to your quilt, if desired.

Bright and Breezy Runner, pieced and quilted by Peta Peace

FINISHED RUNNER: 14½" × 52½" • FINISHED BLOCKS: 8" × 14" and 12" × 14"

Bright and Breezy Runner

There's something so special about the summer: spending time with friends and family at BBQs and parties, staying up way too late, and laughing a lot. It's my favorite time of the year. Somehow there's never quite enough time to sew, though, so a quick project like a table runner is a great way to keep the sewing machine humming while still getting out to enjoy the sun and fun!

Materials

Yardage is based on 42"-wide fabric.

- 11 precut squares, 10" × 10", of assorted prints for blocks
- ⅝ yard of white solid for background
- ⅜ yard of blue print for binding
- 1⅝ yards of fabric for backing*
- 18" × 56" piece of batting

If you prefer a pieced backing, purchase just 1⅛ yards.

Cutting

From *each* of the 11 precut squares, cut:
4 rectangles, 2½" × 9" (44 total)

From the white solid, cut:
4 strips, 4½" × 42"; crosscut into:
    20 squares, 4½" × 4½"
    12 rectangles, 2½" × 4½"

From the blue print, cut:
4 strips, 2½" × 42"

Block A Assembly

Use ¼" seam allowances. Press the seam allowances after each step as indicated by the arrows.

1. Sew seven 2½" × 9" print rectangles together as shown. Trim to 8½" × 14½".

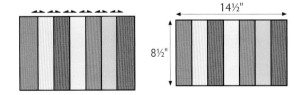

2. Draw a diagonal line from corner to corner on the wrong side of four 4½" white squares. Place two marked squares on diagonally opposite corners of the pieced unit and sew on the lines, referring to "Easy Corner Triangles and Flying Geese" on page 75. Trim ¼" outside the sewn lines. Repeat to attach the remaining squares to the other two corners of the pieced unit. Make two blocks, 8½" × 14½", including the seam allowances.

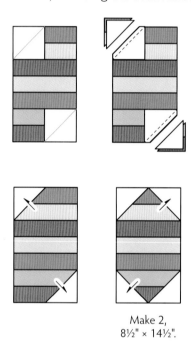

Make 2,
8½" × 14½".

Block B Assembly

1. Sew six 2½" × 9" print rectangles together. Trim to 6½" × 12½".

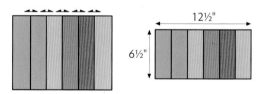

2. Sew two 2½" × 9" print rectangles together as shown. Trim to 4½" × 8½". Make two.

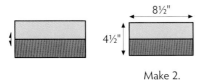

Make 2.

3. Draw a diagonal line from corner to corner on the wrong side of two 4½" white squares. Place one marked square on a pieced unit from step 2, matching the raw edges and orienting the line as shown. Sew on the drawn line. Trim ¼" outside the sewn line. Add the second marked square to the opposite corner in the same way to construct a flying-geese unit. Make two.

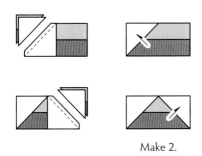

Make 2.

4. Sew a white 2½" × 4½" rectangle to each side of a flying-geese unit. Make two. The units should measure 4½" × 12½", including the seam allowances.

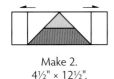

Make 2.
4½" × 12½".

5. Sew the pieced units from step 4 to the long edges of a pieced unit from step 1. Repeat to make three blocks measuring 12½" × 14½", including the seam allowances.

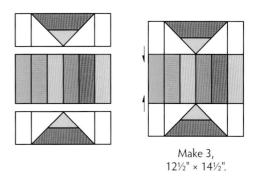

Make 3,
12½" × 14½".

Runner Assembly

Arrange the blocks in a single row, alternating blocks A and B and matching the seam intersections. The completed table-runner top should measure 14½" × 52½".

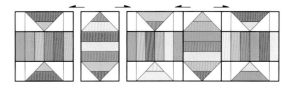

Table-runner assembly

Finishing the Runner

Refer to "Finishing Your Quilt" on page 76 for details as needed.

1. Cut a piece of backing fabric 18" × 56".

2. Layer the quilt top with batting and backing. Baste and quilt as desired. The runner shown is machine quilted with straight lines that are parallel to the short edges of the runner.

3. Bind the edges with the blue 2½"-wide strips. Add a label to your table runner, if desired.

Origami Squares, pieced by Peta Peace and quilted by Diane Farrugia

FINISHED QUILT: 60½" × 60½" • FINISHED BLOCK: 20½" × 20½"

Origami Squares

Since our girls were little, there have been loads of craft and rainy-day activities around our house. Origami is one that keeps making an appearance. Our girls love origami and are definitely better at it than I am! Unlike those tricky bits of folded paper, the Origami Squares quilt is easy to make, and this type of origami will keep you warm! Much better, right?

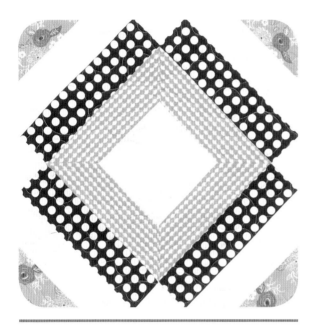

Materials

Yardage is based on 42"-wide fabric.

- 36 precut squares, 10" × 10", of assorted prints for blocks
- 2⅛ yards of white solid for background
- ⅝ yard of pink print for blocks
- ⅝ yard of raspberry print for binding
- 4 yards of fabric for backing
- 68" × 68" piece of batting

Cutting

From *each* of the 36 precut squares, cut:
4 rectangles, 2½" × 9" (144 total)

From the white solid, cut:
9 strips, 2½" × 42"; crosscut into 36 rectangles, 2½" × 9"
3 strips, 5¼" × 42"; crosscut into 36 rectangles, 3" × 5¼"
6 strips, 5¼" × 42"; crosscut into 36 squares, 5¼" × 5¼". Cut each square in half diagonally to yield 72 triangles.

From the pink print, cut:
3 strips, 5¼" × 42"; crosscut into 36 rectangles, 3" × 5¼"

From the raspberry print, cut:
7 strips, 2½" × 42"

Block Assembly

Use ¼" seam allowances. Press the seam allowances after each step as indicated by the arrows.

For each block you will need 16 print rectangles, 2½" × 9" (four each of four prints), four 2½" × 9" white rectangles, four 3" × 5¼" white rectangles, four 3" × 5¼" pink rectangles,

Secondary Patterns

The nine blocks in this quilt are made from matching strips and have white centers. But where the corners of the large blocks come together, scrappy squares with pink centers form. This secondary pattern is a bonus of the block design.

and eight white triangles. As you're sewing, keep the fabric placement the same for all four quarter blocks within one block.

1. Sew two 2½" × 9" print rectangles together side by side. Make a second unit using two different prints. Repeat to make four units in each print combination.

Make 4 of each.

2. Sew pieced units to the sides of a 2½" × 9" white rectangle, using all four prints in each unit. Make four. Trim to measure 8½" × 10½", including the seam allowances.

Make 4 units,
8½" × 10½".

3. Fold a pieced unit in half as shown on page 49 and press gently to crease the center line. Find and mark the centers of a 3" × 5¼" white rectangle and a 3" × 5¼" pink rectangle. Carefully pin the white rectangle to the left edge of the pieced unit, matching

the centers. Sew in place. Repeat to attach the pink rectangle to the right edge of the unit. Make four.

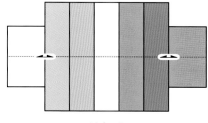

Make 4.

4. Lightly press two white triangles in half as shown. Center the triangles on the long edges of a unit from step 3. Pin and sew with right sides together. Repeat to make four quarter blocks. Press the seam allowances on two of the quarter blocks toward the center and on two of the quarter blocks toward the triangles to ensure that the seams nest when sewing the quarter blocks together. Lightly press each quarter block in half diagonally, if necessary, to renew the centerline creases.

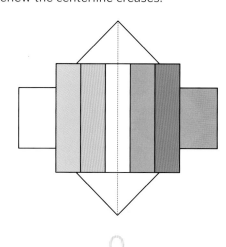

Stretch Control

Handle the cut pieces carefully and use extra pins to prevent the bias edge of each triangle from stretching as you sew.

5. Place one of the quarter blocks on a cutting mat. Align the 45° mark on a rotary-cutting ruler with the block's centerline, and position the center of the block (where the creases intersect) 5¼" from the ruler's right edge. Be sure that the join between the first and second print rectangles is ¼" from the edge of the ruler, as shown below in the circled area. Trim the excess fabric from the right edge of the block.

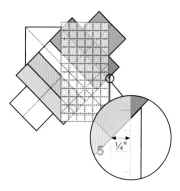
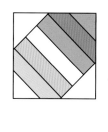

6. Rotate the quarter block 180° and repeat the alignment process. Trim away the excess fabric, leaving the block 10½" wide.

7. Turn the block 90° and repeat steps 5 and 6 to trim the quarter block to 10½" square. Make four quarter blocks.

8. Arrange the four quarter blocks in two rows of two as shown. Remember to position the quarter blocks so that the seam allowances nest together. Sew two rows, pressing the seam allowances in opposite directions. Sew the rows together. Make nine blocks measuring 20½" square, including the seam allowances.

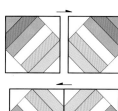
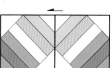
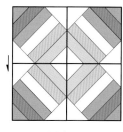

Make 9,
20½" × 20½".

Quilt Assembly

1. Referring to the quilt assembly diagram below, arrange the blocks in three rows of three. Sew each row together. Each row should measure 20½" × 60½", including the seam allowances.

2. Sew the rows together. The quilt top should measure 60½" square.

Finishing the Quilt

Refer to "Finishing Your Quilt" on page 76 for details as needed.

1. Trim the selvages from the backing fabric and cut the backing into two pieces, approximately 42" × 72" each. Prepare the backing as instructed in "Making the Quilt Backing" on page 76. Trim to approximately 68" square to make a backing with a vertical seam.

2. Layer the quilt top with batting and backing. Baste and quilt as desired. The quilt shown is machine quilted with an allover loop design.

3. Bind the edges with the 2½"-wide raspberry strips. Add a label to your quilt, if desired.

Quilt assembly

The Simplest Sampler

I love sampler quilts but if you're anything like me, you've probably started one (or three!) and not finished them. When made from a collection of prints, the Simplest Sampler has the look of a sampler but there's one big difference: it's made with just one block, so it's a dream to piece and finish!

Materials

Yardage is based on 42"-wide fabric.

- 1¾ yards of white solid for blocks
- 36 precut squares, 10" × 10", of assorted prints for blocks
- 2⅛ yards of aqua solid for background, sashing, and border
- ⅝ yard of teal diagonal stripe for binding
- 3¾ yards of fabric for backing
- 67" × 74" piece of batting

Cutting

From the white solid, cut:
6 strips, 3¼" × 42"; crosscut into 72 squares, 3¼" × 3¼"
3 strips, 2½" × 42"; crosscut into 36 squares, 2½" × 2½"
3 strips, 10" × 42"; crosscut into 72 strips, 1½" × 10"

From *each* of the 36 precut squares, cut:
4 squares, 3¼" × 3¼" (144 total)
1 square, 2½" × 2½" (36 total)
2 strips, 1½" × 10" (72 total)
2 squares, 1½" × 1½" (72 total; 16 will be left over)

From the aqua solid, cut:
6 strips, 3¼" × 42"; crosscut into 72 squares, 3¼" × 3¼"
5 strips, 6½" × 42"; crosscut into 127 strips, 1½" × 6½"
7 strips, 2½" × 42"

From the teal diagonal stripe, cut:
7 strips, 2½" × 42"

The Simplest Sampler, pieced by Peta Peace and quilted by Diane Farrugia

FINISHED QUILT: 59½" × 66½" • **FINISHED BLOCK: 6" × 6"**

Block A Assembly

Use ¼" seam allowances. Press the seam allowances after each step as indicated by the arrows.

Use a single print within each block; each print will be used in two blocks (one A block and one B block).

1. Draw a diagonal line from corner to corner on the wrong side of two 3¼" white squares.

2. Place a marked square on a 3¼" print square with right sides together. Pin the white square in place and sew a scant ¼" from the drawn line on both sides. Cut on the drawn line to yield two half-square-triangle units. Make four. Trim to 2½" square, including the seam allowances.

Make 4.

3. Sew a 1½" × 10" white strip to a 1½" × 10" print strip with right sides together. Crosscut the strip set into four segments, 2½" wide.

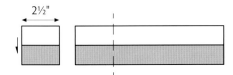

2½"

4. Arrange the four half-square-triangle units, the four strip-set segments, and one 2½" white square as shown. Sew the units together in rows and then join the rows to make a block. Make 36 A blocks measuring 6½" square, including the seam allowances.

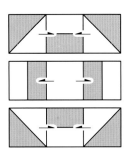 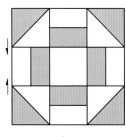

Make 36,
6½" × 6½".

Block B Assembly

Block B is assembled in the same way as block A, with some fabric changes.

1. Repeat step 1, using 3¼" aqua squares in place of white squares.

2. When you assemble the block, use a print square at the center and change the positions of the half-square-triangle units and strip-set segments as shown. Make 36 B blocks measuring 6½" square, including the seam allowances.

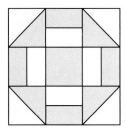

Make 36,
6½" × 6½".

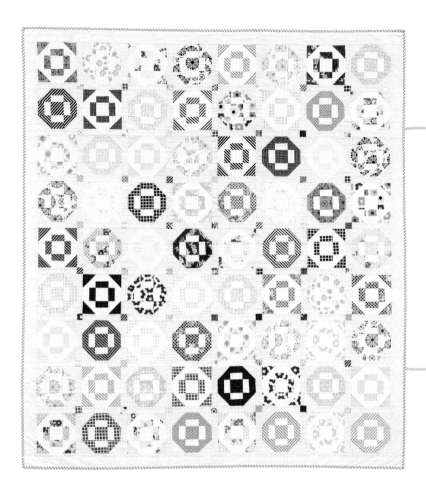

Background Colors

Because I used a white solid in the blocks, I needed the background to be clearly different. A soft aqua was perfect for unifying the blocks. Select your background color based on what works well with the majority of prints in whatever Layer Cake you're using.

Super Stripes

The binding for this quilt was cut from a print featuring diagonal stripes. If you want the same look from a fabric that has straight-grain stripes, cut the binding strips on the bias. You'll need to purchase more fabric, about ⅔ yard, and cut bias strips totaling about 265".

Quilt Assembly

1. Referring to the quilt assembly diagram on page 55, arrange the A and B blocks in nine rows of eight blocks, alternating the A and B blocks. Place aqua 1½" × 6½" strips between blocks in each row. Sew the rows together to measure 6½" × 55½", including the seam allowances.

2. Sew together eight aqua 1½" × 6½" strips and seven 1½" print squares as shown to make a sashing row. Make eight sashing rows measuring 1½" × 55½", including the seam allowances.

3. Sew the rows together. Match the seams and pin at the intersections before sewing. The quilt center should measure 55½" × 62½", including the seam allowances.

Adding the Border

For detailed instructions, refer to "Borders" on page 76.

1. Sew the seven aqua 2½" × 42" strips together end to end to make one long strip. Press the seam allowances open.

2. Cut two strips, 2½" × 62½", and sew them to opposite sides of the quilt center.

3. Cut two strips, 2½" × 59½", and sew them to the top and bottom edges of the quilt. The quilt top should measure 59½" × 66½".

Finishing the Quilt

Refer to "Finishing Your Quilt" on page 76 for details as needed.

1. Trim the selvages from the backing fabric and cut the backing into two pieces, approximately 42" × 67" each. Prepare the backing as instructed in "Making the Quilt Backing" on page 76. Trim to approximately 67" × 74" for a backing with a horizontal seam.

2. Layer the quilt top with batting and backing. Baste and quilt as desired. The quilt shown is quilted with diamond shapes.

3. Bind the edges with the teal striped 2½"-wide strips. Add a label to your quilt, if desired.

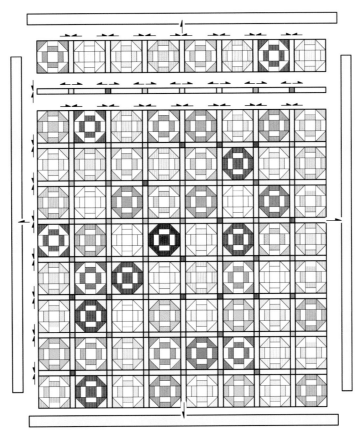

Quilt assembly

Square Peg in a Round Hole, pieced by Peta Peace and quilted by Fiona Bell

FINISHED QUILT: 70½" × 70½" • FINISHED BLOCK: 20" × 20"

Square Peg in a Round Hole

For everyone who has ever felt like the proverbial square peg in a round hole or loved someone like that, this is my way of letting you know that you do fit, in your own beautiful and unique way, and your presence makes the world better.

Materials

Yardage is based on 42"-wide fabric.

- 36 precut squares, 10" × 10", of assorted prints for blocks
- 4¼ yards of white solid for blocks and border
- 3½ yards of raspberry print for appliqué and binding*
- 4½ yards of fabric for backing
- 78" × 78" piece of batting
- 21" × 21" square of freezer paper
- Circle-making tool (optional)
- Removable marking tool

Cutting

From *each* of the 36 precut squares, cut:
6 squares, 3" × 3" (216 total; 36 will be left over)
10 squares, 1¾" × 1¾" (360 total; 171 will be
    left over)

From the white solid, cut:
12 strips, 3" × 42"; crosscut into 144 squares,
    3" × 3"
2 strips, 5½" × 42"; crosscut into 36 strips,
    1¾" × 5½"
2 strips, 6¾" × 42"; crosscut into 36 strips,
    1¾" × 6¾"
2 strips, 8" × 42"; crosscut into 36 strips, 1¾" × 8"
18 strips, 1⅜" × 42"; crosscut *each* strip into 2
    different lengths:
    1 strip, 1⅜" × 19¼" (18 total)
    1 strip, 1⅜" × 21" (18 total)*
7 strips, 5½" × 42"

From the raspberry print, cut:
5 strips, 21" × 42"; crosscut *each* strip into
    2 squares, 21" × 21" (10 total)
8 strips, 2½" × 42"

*If your usable fabric width is less than 42", you can shorten the 21" strips by as much as ½" if necessary. When you piece the blocks, center each shortened strip on the edge of the pieced unit. The corners will be trimmed away during reverse appliqué.

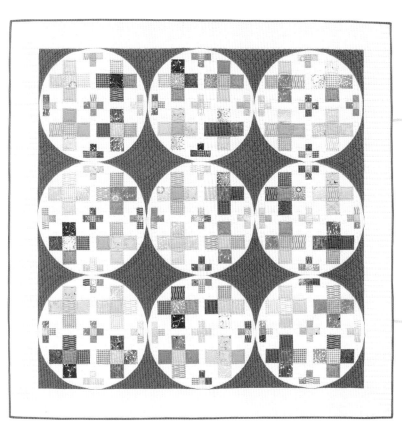

More Is Better

The cutting instructions yield many extra print squares, allowing for flexibility in color placement. Keep the extra squares to use in other projects such as the Square Peg Mini-Quilt on page 63.

Block Assembly

Use ¼" seam allowances. Press the seam allowances after each step as indicated by the arrows.

1. Sort the print pieces by color families or coordinating colors. Choose four sets of five 3" squares for the large crosses, four sets of four 1¾" squares for the edge crosses, and one set of five 1¾" squares for the center cross. Arrange the squares as you would like them to appear in the block, referring to the photo above and the illustrations following step 5 on page 59.

2. Sew five print 3" squares and four white 3" squares together to make a nine-patch unit measuring 8" square, including the seam allowances. Make four.

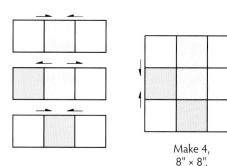

Make 4,
8" × 8".

SASHING ASSEMBLY FOR BLOCKS

1. Following your arrangement of the pieces, sew three print 1¾" squares from the top or bottom cross together and then sew 1¾" × 6¾" white strips to the ends. Make two strips measuring 1¾" × 16¾", including the seam allowances, for the top and bottom sashing rows.

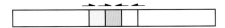

2. Sew three print 1¾" squares from a side cross together and then sew 1¾" × 8" white strips to the ends. Make two strips measuring 1¾" × 19¼", including the seam allowances, for the side sashing.

3. Sew print 1¾" squares to the ends of a white 1¾" × 5½" strip to make a sashing strip. Make four strips measuring 1¾" × 8", including the seam allowances.

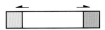

4. Join two sashing strips with the central 1¾" print square from the center cross to make the center sashing strip measuring 1¾" × 16¾", including the seam allowances.

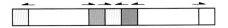

5. Arrange and sew the nine-patch units and sashing strips to make the block center. The block center should measure 19¼" square, including the seam allowances.

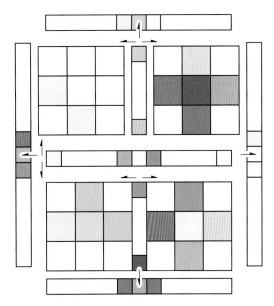

6. To complete the block, sew white 1⅜" × 19¼" strips to the top and bottom edges of the block. Sew white 1⅜" × 21" strips to the sides. The completed block should measure 21" square, including the seam allowances. Make nine blocks with different print combinations in each block.

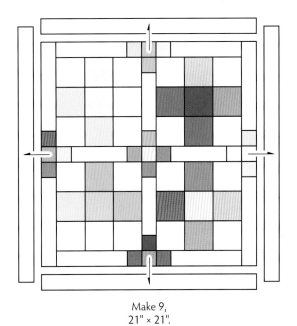

Make 9,
21" × 21".

Pattern Drafting

1. Fold the freezer paper in half lengthwise and crosswise, and finger-press the creases firmly to mark the centerlines. Trace each line with a pencil to permanently mark the creases all the way to the edge.

2. Use a circle-making tool to draw a 20"-diameter circle centered on the freezer paper.

Going Around in Circles

If you don't have a tool for drawing large circles, use a pushpin, a pencil, and a piece of string to make your own compass. Place the freezer paper on a padded surface, such as corrugated cardboard, and insert the pushpin at the center point. Tie one end of the string to the pushpin. Measure 20" from the pushpin and tie the string to the pencil there. Holding the string taut, move the pencil around the pushpin to draw the circle. It may be easier to leave the freezer paper folded and trace just one quarter of the full circle. Cut through the folded paper and unfold it to reveal the complete circle.

3. Carefully cut out the inside of the circle leaving the area outside of the circle intact. You may need to cut slightly inside the drawn line to keep the dimensions accurate. Measure the diameter of the completed circle pattern to ensure that it is 20".

Reverse Appliqué

1. Fold a 21" square of raspberry print in half horizontally and vertically and press to mark the midpoint of each side. Place the square right side up on a heat-resistant surface. Align the pencil marks on the freezer-paper pattern with the center creases on the fabric and press the freezer paper onto the fabric with an iron. Trace lightly around the circle with a removable marking tool.

2. Peel the freezer paper from the fabric and cut out the center of the circle, leaving a ⅜" seam allowance inside the circle. With a pair of small scissors, snip into the seam allowance every ¼" to ⅜", clipping from the raw edge to a point ⅛" inside the drawn line.

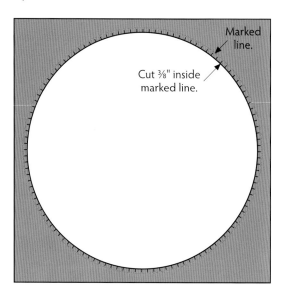

Marked line.

Cut ⅜" inside marked line.

3. Place the square with snipped seam allowance right side up on one of the pieced blocks. Align the centers of each side, making sure that the corners of the block and square are aligned correctly. Pin in place. Replace the freezer-paper circle pattern in the cutout circle to be sure that the circle isn't distorted; make small adjustments as needed. Use lots of pins to secure the circle. Remove the pattern, and then move the work to your ironing board.

4. Spray the snipped seam allowance with starch and turn it under along the drawn line. Work carefully with just a little bit at a time, removing pins and pressing the folded edge as you go. Keep the curve smooth, without points. Replace the pins after pressing so that the circle stays nice and round.

5. Use the pattern to check the circle's shape once again. Make slight adjustments to the fabric and press again if necessary. When you're happy with the circle, and it is secured with pins, edgestitch the circle through all layers to hold the appliqué in place. Use matching thread to blend into the raspberry print.

6. Turn the block over and use a sharp pair of scissors to trim the pieced block and excess raspberry seam allowance, leaving ¼" seam allowance outside the circle. Be very careful not to cut through the raspberry print around the circle on the right side of the block.

7. Press the block from the right side, and then trim the completed block to 20½" square,

centering the circle and leaving ¼" seam allowance at each side. Make nine blocks.

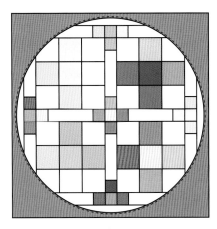

Make 9,
20½" × 20½".

Quilt Assembly

1. Referring to the quilt assembly diagram on page 62, sew three blocks together to make one row as shown. Make three rows. Each row should measure 20½" × 60½", including the seam allowances.

2. Sew the rows together to complete the quilt center. The completed quilt center should measure 60½" square, including the seam allowances.

Adding the Border

For detailed instructions, refer to "Borders" on page 76.

1. Sew the white 5½" × 42" strips together end to end to make one long strip. Press the seam allowances open.

2. Cut two strips, 5½" × 60½", and sew them to opposite sides of the quilt center.

3. Cut two strips, 5½" × 70½", and sew them to the top and bottom edges of the quilt. The quilt top should measure 70½" × 70½".

Finishing the Quilt

Refer to "Finishing Your Quilt" on page 76 for details as needed.

1. Trim the selvages from the backing fabric and cut the backing into two pieces, approximately 42" × 81" each. Prepare the backing as instructed in "Making the Quilt Backing" on page 76. Trim to approximately 78" square for a backing with a horizontal seam.

2. Layer the quilt top with batting and backing. Baste and quilt as desired. The quilt shown is quilted with overlapping circles in the blocks and a curved grid design in the background.

3. Bind the edges with the raspberry 2½"-wide strips. Add a label to your quilt, if desired.

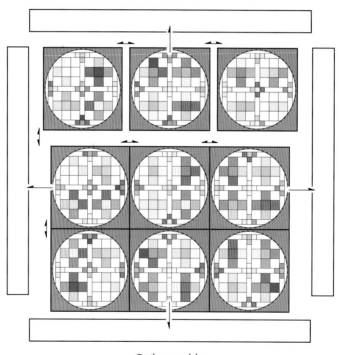

Quilt assembly

Square Peg Mini-Quilt

Mini-quilts are all the rage, and they're a great quick project when time is short. This is a true scrap project, ideally suited for using small leftover bits from previous quilts such as Square Peg in a Round Hole.

Materials

Yardage is based on 42"-wide fabric. Fat quarters measure 18" × 21".

- Leftovers, at least 2½" × 2½", from precut squares for blocks*
- 1 fat quarter of white solid for background
- 1 fat quarter of charcoal stripe for binding
- 1 fat quarter of fabric for backing
- 18" × 18" piece of batting

*You could also use scraps. Group leftover squares or scraps by color, using the photograph on page 64 as a guide. You'll need at least five pieces per color.

Cutting

From the leftover squares, cut:
20 squares, 2½" × 2½" (5 *each* of 4 color families)
21 squares, 1½" × 1½" (5 of the center color family,
    3 *each* of 4 additional color families, and 4
    assorted squares)

From the white solid, cut:
2 strips, 2½" × 21"; crosscut into 16 squares,
    2½" × 2½"
4 strips, 1½" × 21"; crosscut into:
    4 strips, 1½" × 4½"
    4 strips, 1½" × 5½"
    4 strips, 1½" × 6½"

From the backing fabric, cut:
1 square, 18" × 18"

From the charcoal stripe, cut:
4 strips, 2½" × 21"

Square Peg Mini-Quilt, pieced and quilted by Peta Peace

FINISHED QUILT: 15½" × 15½" • FINISHED BLOCK: 6" × 6"

Block Assembly

Use ¼" seam allowances. Press the seam allowances after each step as indicated by the arrows.

Sew five 2½" print squares and four 2½" white solid squares together to make a Nine Patch block measuring 6½" square, including the seam allowances. Make four.

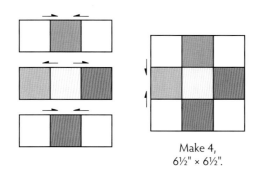

Make 4,
6½" × 6½".

Quilt Assembly

1. Referring to the quilt assembly diagram above right, arrange the blocks, white sashing strips, and print 1½" squares as shown.

2. Join the 1½" squares and white sashing strips as shown. Press.

3. Sew a short sashing strip between each pair of Nine Patch blocks to make two rows. Join the rows with the center sashing strip.

4. Stitch the top and bottom sashing strips to the quilt. Sew the side sashing strips to the quilt sides. The mini-quilt top should measure 15½" square.

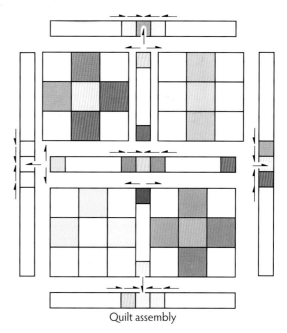

Quilt assembly

Finishing the Mini-Quilt

Refer to "Finishing Your Quilt" on page 76 for details as needed.

1. Layer the quilt top with batting and backing. Baste and quilt as desired. The quilt shown is quilted with concentric circles/arcs around a diagonal grid. For quilting tips, see "Quilting Circles" at left.

2. Bind the edges with the 2½"-wide charcoal strips. Add a label to your mini-quilt, if desired.

Surprise, pieced by Peta Peace and quilted by Diane Farrugia

FINISHED QUILT: 56" × 71" • FINISHED BLOCK: 9" × 9"

Before I started quilting, I had a bit of a reputation for fancy gift wrapping. These days, time gets away from me and the wrapping isn't quite as pretty. Surprise is my new wrapping style—in a quilt! Make this design for someone special as a birthday gift or use Christmas prints for a holiday quilt.

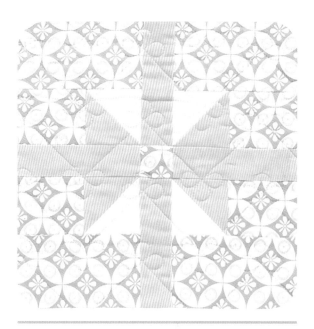

Materials

Yardage is based on 42"-wide fabric.

- 2 yards of white solid for blocks and sashing
- ¾ yard of pink solid for ribbons
- ¾ yard of gray solid for ribbons
- 30 precut squares, 10" × 10", of assorted prints for blocks
- ⅝ yard of green print for binding
- 3⅝ yards of fabric for backing
- 64" × 79" piece of batting

Cutting

From the white solid, cut:
5 strips, 3" × 42"; crosscut into 60 squares, 3" × 3"
2 strips, 9½" × 42"; crosscut into:
    30 rectangles, 2¼" × 9½"
    1 rectangle, 6½" × 9½"
1 strip, 6½" × 42"; crosscut into 4 rectangles,
    6½" × 9½"
11 strips, 2¼" × 42"

From the pink solid, cut:
3 strips, 3" × 42"; crosscut into 30 squares, 3" × 3"
3 strips, 4½" × 42"; crosscut into 60 rectangles,
    1½" × 4½"

From the gray solid, cut:
3 strips, 3" × 42"; crosscut into 30 squares, 3" × 3"
3 strips, 4½" × 42"; crosscut into 60 rectangles,
    1½" × 4½"

From *each* of the 30 precut squares, cut:
4 rectangles, 2¾" × 4½" (120 total)
4 rectangles, 2¼" × 2¾" (120 total)
1 square, 1½" × 1½" (30 total)

From the green print, cut:
7 strips, 2½" × 42"

It's a Wrap

Surprise could become a fun seek-and-find quilt for a young recipient. Use an assortment of novelty fabrics featuring animals, cartoons, or characters from books and movies as the package wrappings, coordinating each with its own solid-color bow.

Half-Square-Triangle Units

Use ¼" seam allowances. Press the seam allowances after each step as indicated by the arrows.

Refer to "Half-Square Triangles" on page 74 for details as needed.

1. Draw a diagonal line from corner to corner on the wrong side of each 3" white square.

2. Place a marked square on a 3" pink square with right sides together. Pin the white square in place and sew a scant ¼" from the drawn line on both sides. Cut on the drawn line to

yield two half-square-triangle units. Trim to 2¼" square, including the seam allowances. Make 60.

3. Place a marked square on a 3" gray square with right sides together. Repeat step 2 to make 60 half-square-triangle units, 2¼" square, including the seam allowances.

Block Assembly

Use a single print in each block.

1. Sew a print 2¼" × 2¾" rectangle to a gray half-square-triangle unit. Sew a print 2¾" × 4½" rectangle to the top of the unit, paying careful attention to the orientation of the pieces. Make two units, 4½" square, including the seam allowances.

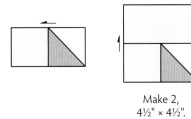

Make 2,
4½" × 4½".

2. Repeat step 1, placing the half-square-triangle unit in the lower-left corner, Make two units, 4½" square, including the seam allowances.

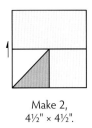

Make 2,
4½" × 4½".

3. Sew gray 1½" × 4½" rectangles to opposite sides of a 1½" print square to make a 1½" × 9½" ribbon unit, including the seam allowances.

4. Sew a step 1 unit to the left edge and a step 2 unit to the right edge of a gray 1½" × 4½" rectangle. Make two units, 4½" × 9½", including the seam allowances.

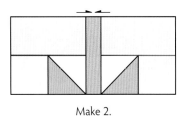

Make 2.

5. Sew the half blocks to the long edges of the ribbon unit from step 3 as shown. Make 15 blocks, 9½" square, including the seam allowances. Repeat the entire process substituting pink pieces for gray to make 15 blocks with pink ribbons.

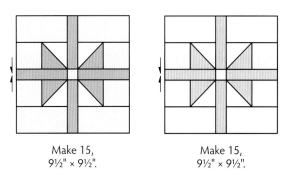

Make 15,
9½" × 9½".

Make 15,
9½" × 9½".

Quilt Assembly

1. Referring to the quilt assembly diagram on page 70, arrange the blocks, white 6½" × 9½" rectangles, and white 2¼" × 9½" rectangles into five rows of six blocks as shown and join the pieces in each row. Each row should measure 9½" × 71", including the seam allowances.

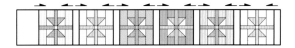

2. Sew the 11 white 2¼" × 42" strips together end to end to make one long strip. Press the seam allowances open. From the pieced strip, cut six sashing strips, 2¼" × 71".

3. Sew the 2¼" × 71" strips between the vertical rows of blocks and along the side edges of the quilt top. Press the seam allowances toward the blocks. The completed quilt top should measure 56" × 71".

Finishing the Quilt

Refer to "Finishing Your Quilt" on page 76 for details as needed.

1. Trim the selvages from the backing fabric and cut the backing into two pieces, approximately 42" × 65" each. Prepare the backing as instructed in "Making the Quilt Backing" on page 76. Trim to approximately 64" × 79" to make a backing with a horizontal seam.

2. Layer the quilt top with batting and backing. Baste and quilt as desired. The quilt shown is quilted with chevrons with loops at the peaks and valleys.

3. Bind the edges with the 2½"-wide green strips. Add a label to your quilt, if desired.

Quilt assembly

Basic Tools and Techniques

When I made my first quilt 15 years ago, I bought a half yard each of 25 prints because a fat quarter of each just didn't sound like enough, and I cut the whole thing out with a pair of fabric scissors. It wasn't that rotary cutters didn't exist (I'm not that old!), it's just that I didn't know about them.

A lot has changed since I made that first quilt, and along the way I've picked up a few tips about quiltmaking and the tools needed. Some tips came from seasoned quilters whom I admire, and some I figured out myself along the way. This section covers those tips. If you're new to quilting, read on; I hope that I can save you time and you'll be less frustrated by imperfect points and wobbly borders than I was in those early days. If you've been quilting for a while, you might want to dive right into the projects, but remember that the tips will be here if you want to take a look later on.

Essential Supplies

Making a quilt is so much easier when you have basic equipment. Before jumping in and buying a ton of fabric as I did, set yourself up for success with the following tools.

ROTARY-CUTTING MAT

Cutting mats come in many sizes and shapes. You don't need to have a particularly large cutting mat, but it is worth investing in one that can fit a half yard of fabric folded in half. An 18" × 24" cutting mat will do that just fine.

ROTARY CUTTER

A good rotary cutter makes life easier, and it's essential for ensuring that the beautiful fabric you've chosen is cut accurately. Rotary cutters are super sharp. Develop the habit of closing the blade cover whenever you put the cutter down, and be careful when changing the blade. Rotary-cutting blades don't last forever; if you find that you need a lot of pressure to make a cut or if your cuts are ragged, it's time for a new one.

ROTARY-CUTTING RULER

When it comes to quilting rulers, there are literally hundreds to choose from, and determining what you need can be overwhelming. If you love quilting, you'll find your ruler collection growing over the years, but to start I recommend a 6" × 24" ruler with clear markings at ¼" intervals.

SEAM RIPPER

No matter how advanced your sewing skills, there will be times when you need to use a seam ripper, so be sure you have a good one (or two!) handy. I like the ones that have a rubber cap to help remove loose threads after I've taken out the stitches.

PINS AND SCISSORS

Because pinning helps ensure accuracy, it's important to have a healthy supply of pins available. If you plan on doing your own machine quilting, you'll also need safety pins for basting the quilt; the curved ones are great for the job. Remember to discard pins of either kind if you feel them catching on the fabric or if they start to look tarnished or bent.

A small, comfortable pair of scissors is also essential; keep them beside your sewing machine for trimming threads while sewing.

SEWING MACHINE AND NEEDLES

A sewing machine is the most important and expensive piece of equipment you'll need for making a quilt. If you don't already have a sewing machine, look for one that has a good straight stitch and, if possible, a walking foot for machine quilting. A ¼" presser foot is almost essential for piecing, and it may come standard with the machine.

Be kind to your sewing machine. Give it a good cleaning and change the needle after every quilt. You should also have it serviced by an authorized technician at least once a year (or more often if you sew a lot).

Squaring Up and Cutting Fabric

Working with precut fabric greatly reduces the amount of squaring up you'll need to do to make the quilts in this book, but squaring up is still a handy skill. You'll need it for cutting background yardage, borders, and so on.

Selvage Sense

Selvages are the finished edges of the fabric, usually printed with the name of the designer and manufacturer. Remove the selvages before using the fabric.

Fold the fabric yardage in half, aligning the selvages, and place the fabric on your cutting mat with the selvages parallel to the horizontal lines. Smooth out the fabric with your hand and double-check the alignment again; then place a ruler along one edge of the fabric, aligned with a vertical grid line on the cutting mat, and cut off the uneven fabric end.

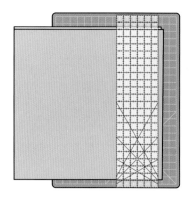

Cut strips of the desired width, starting from the squared edge. Rotate the fabric and mat together to position them correctly for cutting. After every few strips, take a minute to check that the cut is still perpendicular to the fold. If not, make a new cut to square it up.

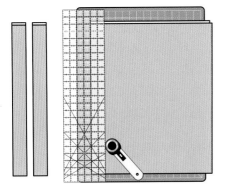

To cut squares or rectangles, cut a strip in the appropriate width, and then rotate the strip 90°. Square up the strip end; then cut squares or rectangles to the desired dimensions.

What About Those Pinked Edges?

The pinked edges found on precut fabrics aren't just there to look pretty. They're designed to stop the fabric from fraying before it is used. It's a great idea, but it can be a little confusing to work out how to treat the pinked edge when sewing.

The best bet is to measure the precut squares as soon as you open the package. Then you'll know whether to align your ruler with the tip or the dip of the pinked edge. Don't worry too much; for the projects in this book, you'll divide the precut squares and trim away most of the pinked edges.

The Perfect ¼" Seam Allowance

An accurate seam allowance is vitally important in quilting. Get it right and piecing is a dream, but even a little variance means that your blocks won't end up the right size, points may be cut off, pieces may not align correctly, and you may end up frustrated.

The perfect ¼" seam allowance in quilting is actually a *scant* ¼". Using a ¼" presser foot on your sewing machine will help you achieve this, but it's worth checking to be sure that the seam-allowance width is accurate on your machine when using your ¼" presser foot. Align the edge of a fabric scrap with the guide edge of the ¼" presser foot, sew the seam, and then measure the seam allowance with a ruler. The stitches should lie just inside the ¼" mark on the ruler. If they're on or outside of the ¼" mark, change the needle position by a tiny increment (if your machine has that function) or move the fabric very slightly away from the presser foot's guide as the fabric passes underneath the needle.

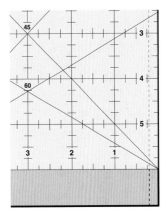

Pinning Is Winning!

Pinning makes sewing faster because you're not struggling to keep the pieces aligned as you sew, and it really does make all the difference in getting clean points and joins. I don't think there's any such thing as overpinning, but as a general rule I place at least one pin at each end of a short seam (less than 4"). On longer seams I pin through every seam intersection as well as at the ends of the seam.

Pressing

In every project in this book you'll need to press the seam allowances before moving on to the next step. Be sure your iron is hot and place the iron on the seam to set the stitches. Open the fabric pieces with your fingers or the tip of the iron and press the seam allowances as directed, usually to one side. Be careful not to slide the iron around; doing so will distort the fabric, leading to difficulty in the next steps of piecing. Instead, lift and replace the iron to press the entire seam. In other words: press, don't iron.

Chain Piecing

Chain piecing is a great way to speed up your quiltmaking. Simply sew pairs of pieces together one after another without stopping to cut the threads between units. Snip the threads between units after all of the pieces have been sewn. Chain piecing saves time and reduces the amount of thread you use—a double bonus!

Triangles! Triangles! Triangles!

Triangles are used often in quilt patterns. They are a staple of quiltmaking and have been for hundreds of years, but they can be intimidating. There are quite a few methods for making half-square-triangle units and flying geese, but the following are my favorites because they're easy, and I think they produce the best results.

HALF-SQUARE TRIANGLES

1. Draw a diagonal line from corner to corner on the wrong side of a fabric square. Place the marked square on top of a second square of fabric, right sides together.

2. Sew a scant ¼" from the drawn line on both sides of the line.

3. Cut on the drawn line to yield two half-square-triangle units. Press each unit as directed and then trim to the exact size required.

To trim the half-square-triangle units, place a rotary-cutting ruler on the pressed unit with its 45° line along the seam and cut along two edges as shown. Rotate the pieced unit 180°, replace the ruler, and trim the remaining two edges.

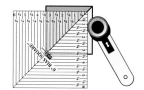 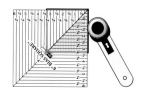

Tools That Rule

For trimming half-square-triangle units to the desired size, I use a Bloc Loc Half-Square-Triangle Ruler. It makes life super easy—trust me, this ruler is life changing! It's available in a whole range of sizes, but the 4½" size is perfect for the projects in this book.

Now that you have perfect half-square-triangle units, you'll want to make sure you sew them into your blocks perfectly. When I first pieced quilts, I often messed up the triangle's corners until I realized that popping a pin across the diagonal seam makes a world of difference. It helps keep the layers of fabric nicely aligned as you sew, and it means that you won't chop off the point of the triangle when you add the next patch. Take a look at the illustration and give it a try as you work through the projects in this book.

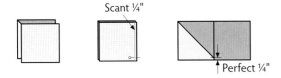

EASY CORNER TRIANGLES AND FLYING GEESE

1. Draw a diagonal line from corner to corner on the wrong side of a fabric square. Place the marked square on top of a rectangle, right sides together, aligning the raw edges as shown in the illustration following step 3.

2. Pin the square in place and sew directly on the drawn line.

3. Trim ¼" outside the drawn line. Press the seam allowances as instructed.

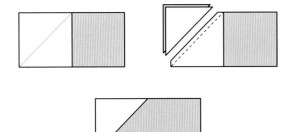

4. To make a flying-geese unit, sew another marked square to the opposite corner of the rectangle as shown.

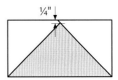

These methods are easy, but if your triangles appear less than perfect try the following tips:

- Practice with scrap fabric. Just as learning to sew with a perfect ¼" seam allowance takes practice, sewing on a line also takes practice.

- Spend a little time making sure that the marked square is accurately and squarely aligned with the rectangle. On larger pieces, I find it helpful to pin the top corner. Also be sure that the pins at the ends of the seamline are as close to the corners as possible.

- Be sure that you have pressed the seam allowances correctly. Sometimes the seam needs a little more pressing to get it right. Remember: press, don't iron.

- If you still find that your easy corner triangle looks more "whoops" than "correct," you may need to adjust where you place the stitching line. Cotton thread comes in several different weights and, if you're sewing with a heavier or thicker thread, you may need to allow for the extra thickness by sewing beside the drawn line rather than on it.

 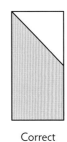 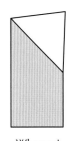

Correct   Whoops!

Finishing Your Quilt

A few techniques are used to complete every quilt. For more information on any of these techniques, visit ShopMartingale.com/HowtoQuilt.

Borders

I don't think I've ever heard any quilters say that adding borders is their favorite part of the quiltmaking process. Adding borders is definitely my least favorite thing to do! I just remember that once the borders are done, the quilt top is finished and just about ready to be loved, so the borders must be worth the effort. If you take your time and follow these steps, you'll be sure to have lovely, straight borders to frame your beautiful work.

I like to sew all the border pieces together end to end to make one long strip. Doing so is much easier than working out the exact size of pieces to join for each border and generally means less fabric is wasted.

Mark the center of each border and each side of the quilt top with pins. Pin the first side border in place by first matching the center pins and then aligning both ends. Add more pins to secure the border to the quilt, pinning about every 3" and distributing the fabric as evenly as possible. Sew the border in place. Press and repeat to attach the second border to the opposite side of the quilt. Pin, sew, and press the remaining borders as before.

Making the Quilt Backing

Cut two equal lengths from the yardage specified in the project instructions, trim the selvage from one side of each piece, and then sew the two pieces together along the trimmed edges. Press the seam allowances open and you're ready to make the quilt sandwich.

The yardage specified for backing in each project (except the small projects) allows an additional 4" of backing around each side of the quilt. The yardage can be reduced slightly if you prefer, but you'll need to allow at least 2" to 3" beyond the quilt top on all sides. If you're planning to have your project quilted by a long-arm quilter, check with your quilter to be sure you include the additional backing required.

Batting

I prefer the look and feel of a low-loft 100% cotton batting for my quilts, but there's no right or wrong answer with batting. Talk to your local quilt shop about the different options available and purchase something that will suit the style of your quilt and the climate you live in.

Making a Quilt Sandwich

1. Lay the quilt backing right side down on a large flat surface (your floor is perfect) and smooth it out so that there are no wrinkles. Use small pieces of masking tape to hold the corners and sides in place. The backing fabric should be taut but not stretched.

2. Place the batting on top of the backing and smooth out any wrinkles with your hands. I like to start in one corner and work my way down and across the batting.

3. Place the quilt top right side up on top of the batting and smooth out any wrinkles. Be sure that the quilt top is centered and has at least 2" of batting and backing around all sides.

4. Starting in the center of the quilt, use curved safety pins through all three layers to baste the quilt. Place the pins no more than a hand's width apart to keep the layers from shifting as you quilt.

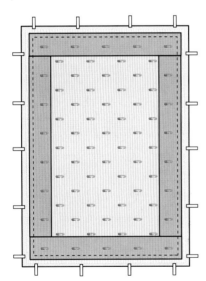

Quilting

There are several options for quilting your project. I send a lot of my quilts out to be professionally quilted on a long-arm machine, but I still enjoy sitting down and doing quilting myself when time allows.

- HAND QUILTING. Believe it or not, I hand quilted every quilt I made for 12 years! It's relaxing to hand quilt while watching a movie, and it doesn't require any special equipment apart from a good needle and quilting thread.

- MACHINE-GUIDED QUILTING. Straight-line quilting on your home sewing machine is definitely faster than hand quilting, and it's fun. You'll need a walking foot so that all three layers of the quilt feed through the machine evenly. Stitch slowly and you'll find that something that looks intimidating is actually quite easy and fun.

- FREE-MOTION QUILTING. I use an open-toe free-motion foot and always warm up by stitching on a little test quilt sandwich made with scraps of fabric and batting before I start on the quilt. I find that doing so gets my hands, feet, and brain in sync, and I get a better, more even result on the quilt. If you're new to free-motion quilting, I suggest you find a class or book on the subject to help you on the journey!

Binding

I use double-fold binding on all of my quilts and prefer to hand stitch the binding to the back of the quilt. I think it's a throwback to my hand-quilting days, and it gives me a chance to catch up on movies and television shows I've saved. Sewing the binding is hands down my favorite part of making a quilt.

I cut my binding 2¼" wide, which is a little narrower than the standard 2½" strips, because I like a narrower binding. The measurements given in each project are for standard 2½"-wide binding strips, but you might like to give my preference a try. It looks especially good on smaller quilts.

1. Trim away excess batting and backing, leaving an extra ⅛" of batting and backing beyond the quilt. This will help ensure that the binding is full and even on both the front and back of the quilt.

2. Cut the number of binding strips specified in the project and then trim off the selvages. With right sides together, sew the strips together end to end to make one long strip. Press the seam allowances open.

3. Press the long binding strip in half, wrong sides together.

4. Pin one end of the binding to the right side of the quilt, aligning the raw edge of the binding with the raw edge of the quilt top. Don't align it with the edge of the batting! Position the end of the binding away from a corner, in an inconspicuous part of the quilt.

5. Leaving a 5" tail free at the beginning of the binding, stitch the binding to the quilt. Sew through all three layers using a ¼" seam allowance, measured from the binding raw edge.

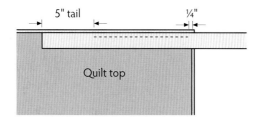

6. Stop sewing ¼" from the first corner and backstitch. Remove the quilt from the machine and fold the binding up so the fold forms a 45° angle. Hold the first fold in place and fold the binding back down so that it's aligned with the next side of the quilt top. Start stitching again at the edge of the quilt. Repeat around all four sides of the quilt.

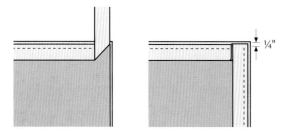

7. When you return to the first side, stop sewing at least 5" from the beginning of the binding. Remove the quilt from the machine and lay it flat on your sewing table. Trim the end of the binding so that it overlaps the beginning by ½".

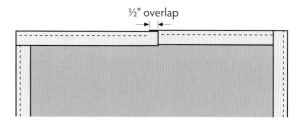

8. Open the folds in both binding ends and pin them together, right sides together. Stitch together with a ¼" seam. Finger-press the seam allowances open.

9. Refold the binding and finish sewing it to the quilt.

10. Wrap the folded edge of the binding over the raw edges to the back of the quilt. Hand stitch the folded edge to the backing, covering the seam and mitering the corners as you go.

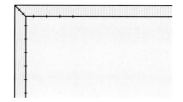

Acknowledgments

Thanks to my family, my husband, Richard, and our daughters, Georgia and Shelby. This book would never have happened without your love and support. Thank you for the endless cups of tea, junk food snacks, washing, and ironing, for cooking dinners, bringing in YouTube videos that aren't that funny, watching reruns of *Glee* that are (and singing along at the top of your lungs), keeping my pin bowl tidy so that I don't stick myself, and for your patience and the absolute lack of complaints about the loose threads that seem to magically migrate from the sewing room to the rest of the house! You three make my heart smile every single day and I love you.

Also, very special thanks to:

- Cathie—there will never be enough words to express just how grateful I am that you flew up here to help me cut, pin, press, and sew for a whole week. Thank you.

- Mum and Dad for the school pickups, chocolate deliveries, everything you taught me (especially the pinning, Mum!), and for all you do that lets me do this quilty thing.

- Granny, who passed away while I was writing this book, for being the strongest, most passionate, determined, and inspiring role model in my life.

- Lissa and the team at Moda Fabrics and everyone at Ella Blue Fabrics for the beautiful fabrics you provided to help make this book. Also thanks for the support and encouragement you provide to quilters everywhere.

- Everyone at Martingale for giving me the opportunity to write a book about something I love so much and for all of your work and guidance along the way.

- And finally, to the Australian Army for sending us to live 2,500 miles away from my hometown with a 17-day-old baby. What felt like the worst thing ever turned out to be better than anything I could have ever dreamed of. I'm grateful every day that you provided the opportunity and time to make that first quilt and for the kind, supportive, and all-around awesome friends I have because of you.

About the Author

Growing up in a household where stray threads and piles of fabric were as much a part of the furniture as chairs and tables, designer Peta Peace unsurprisingly followed in her mother's and grandmother's footsteps with a love of all things handmade. Over the years she has dabbled in garment and home-decor sewing, but it wasn't until her first daughter was born that the quilting bug took hold.

Fast-forward a few years: most days you will find Peta either at her computer dreaming up new designs or at her sewing machine doing what she loves best: making quilts that she hopes will encourage and inspire people everywhere to give this fabulous craft a try.

You can follow along with her quilting journey on her blog and website, SheQuiltsaLot.com.